M T

before

AMELIA EARHART

Richard Tames

Franklin Watts

London ● New York ● Sydney ● Toronto

Contents

© Franklin Watts

First published in Great Britain
 1989 by
Franklin Watts
96 Leonard Street
London EC2

First published in the USA by
Franklin Watts Inc.
387 Park Avenue South
New York
N.Y. 10016

First published in Australia by
Franklin Watts
14 Mars Road
Lane Cove
NSW 2066

UK ISBN: 0 86313 892 6
US ISBN: 0-531-10851-3
Library of Congress Catalog Card Number: 89-14792

Phototypeset by: JB Type, Hove, East Sussex
Printed in: Belgium
Series Editor: Penny Horton
Designed by: Ross George

Amelia Earhart flew into history through her skill and courage as a flyer. For a whole generation of women she stood for freedom, daring and success. Yet there was nothing in her birth or early life to suggest an extraordinary destiny of fame and fortune.

In 1897, Amelia Earhart was born in the small town of Atchison on the vast plains of Kansas, where there is only flat land and immense sky. Her family, on both sides, were German in origin, who left the old country to settle, at first, in Pennsylvania. Then they moved west on to the prairies in the middle years of the nineteenth century as the building of the railways opened up the land for **cultivation** and settlement.

Amelia and her sister, Grace Muriel, who was three years younger, were brought up in Kansas City but made frequent visits to their grandparents' home in Atchison, where Amelia was born.

Above: **An approved portrait shows Amelia relaxed and cheerful.**

Left: **The endless and fertile plains of Kansas.**

In 1907, when Amelia was ten years old, her father got an office job, working for the Rock Island Railroad in Des Moines, Iowa. Amelia's mother went to join Mr Earhart immediately, to set up a new home. After a year in their grandparents' home, the girls also moved on to Iowa, where Amelia went to a local school.

Iowa was meant to be a fresh start for the Earhart family, but Amelia's father was not destined for success. He was a kind and loving man but too fond of drinking with his friends. In the end his drinking cost him his

Engine storage sheds and turntable of an Iowa railroad station.

job and the family fell on hard times. In 1913 he managed to get another position, with the Great Northern Railway and the Earharts moved on again to St Paul, Minnesota. However, Mr Earhart's new job was poorly paid and the family had to watch every penny. So the girls learned to enjoy themselves by entertainment that cost little or nothing – making their own music and reading books borrowed from the public library.

When Mr Earhart decided to try his luck again in Kansas City, Mrs Earhart and the girls moved to Chicago, where Amelia finally graduated from high school in June 1916, aged 19. Shortly afterwards one of her grandmothers died, leaving both girls some money which enabled them to continue their education. Amelia enrolled in the Ogontz School in Rydal, Pennsylvania, while Muriel chose to go to the Canadian city of Toronto.

In December 1917, Amelia went to spend Christmas with her sister. The United States had just entered World War I and the country was full of enthusiasm. But Canada, as a part of the British Empire, had been in the struggle since 1914. Its hospitals were full of wounded men, **convalescing**. Acting on impulse, Amelia decided to give up her studies and become a Red Cross volunteer. She was sent to Spadina Military Hospital in Ontario, where she was soon given responsible jobs, preparing food in the kitchen for patients with special diets, and handing out prescriptions in the hospital's **dispensary**.

Quite a change from Kansas! – the crowded city of Chicago.

Naturally, Amelia listened to the patients talking about the war in Europe. Stories of their adventures in far away places fed her own restlessness. Above all she was fascinated by the exploits of the men of the Royal Flying Corps, the daring pilots who had taken war up into the sky. Amelia longed to fly and nearby, at Armor Heights, there was an airfield. But military regulations prevented her from doing so.

In the course of 1918 Amelia herself became a patient, struck down by **pneumonia**. To convalesce, she went to stay with her sister who had moved to Northampton, Massachusetts, where she was studying to enter Smith College. Here Amelia spent nearly a year, restless as ever and apparently with no clear idea in her mind about what she should do with her life. She read poetry; played the banjo; went hiking; studied mechanics, and finally enrolled at Columbia University, intending to take a course in medicine. She also took a course in French poetry "for fun".

After a year she went out to Los Angeles to visit her parents and it was in California, at Glendale, that she made her first flight, piloted by the record-breaking Frank Hawks. She never went back to college. Suddenly, Amelia Earhart knew just what she wanted to do with her life.

Right: **Frank Hawks, who piloted the aeroplane that took Amelia into the air for the first time.**

Above: **War in the air. The last example of single combat in modern times.**

The First Flyers

The first ever powered aeroplane flight was made by Orville Wright at Kill Devil Hills, Kitty Hawk, North Carolina, at 10.35a.m. on 17 December 17 December 1903. The flight lasted for 12 seconds at about 48 kilometres (30 miles) per hour, some three metres (ten feet) above the ground. The total distance travelled was less than the length of the cabin of a modern jumbo jet.

Progress in aviation was astonishingly rapid. By 1906 the Wright brothers were flying distances of 80 kilometres (50 miles). In 1907 the world's first aerodrome, complete with **hangars**, opened in France. The following year the world's first flying club, the Aeronautical Society of New York, was founded. In 1909 the world's first flying display was held in France and in the same year the Frenchman

Orville Wright pilots *Flyer* into the pages of history.

8

Louis Blériot flew across the English Channel in 37 minutes. 1910 saw the testing of the world's first seaplane, in France again. In 1911 the British Post Office started the world's first airmail service, although the distance covered, from Hendon to Windsor, was only about 32 kilometres (20 miles). 1912 saw the first use of aeroplanes in warfare and in the same year the first ever flight over 160 kilometres (100 miles) per hour was achieved.

In 1913, the Frenchman Adolphe Pegoud became the first pilot to loop the loop and the first person to jump from an aeroplane using a parachute. In 1914 the world's first regular passenger air service began, flying people, one at a time, across Tampa Bay in Florida.

World War I (1914–18) greatly accelerated the development of aircraft, which were first of all used for **reconnaissance**, then as bombers, and finally as fighters to attack or protect other types of aeroplane. Engines became lighter, more powerful and more reliable and in 1915 the Germans tested the first all-metal aircraft.

By 1919 the British aviators, Alcock and Brown, were able to fly their Vickers Vimy bomber from Newfoundland, Canada, to Ireland in 16 hours and 27 minutes, making the world's first non-stop transatlantic crossing by aeroplane just 15 years after the Wright brothers' first great adventure.

An aeroplane designed by Blériot is put through its paces at an air show.

A Shining Adventure

Amelia's first flight was, in her own words, an experience of "breathtaking beauty". Nothing would stop her from learning to fly herself. After taking private lessons from a pioneer woman pilot, Neta Snook, Amelia made her first solo flight in June 1921. The aeroplane was a Kinner Airster. Later that same year she was to crash land in a cabbage patch. She told her friends that the accident had put her off cabbages, but not flying.

Thirteen months after making her first solo flight Amelia bought her first aeroplane, a Kinner Canary. It was a present to herself on her 25th birthday and it cost her all the money she had saved from her job with a telephone company and what she could raise by **pawning** her few valuable possessions.

Almost as soon as she had acquired her own aeroplane, she set a world altitude record for women, flying to a height of 4,267 kilometres

Bill Kinner with a 1936 folding-wing model of his own design

(14,000 feet). It was an incredibly daring achievement for a **novice**, but Amelia shrugged it off, saying,

"I really wouldn't have cared about the record except it may help Bill Kinner sell his planes."

In the early 1920s flying was very much a matter of bravery. Most flyers were war **veterans**, used to pushing themselves to the limit. **Crop dusting** and mail runs brought in the money, but they did not make exciting flying. For thrills they turned to stunt flying at casually organized "air shows", looping the loop or flying upside down before the upturned gaze of admiring crowds. Amelia soon became a familiar figure at such events.

Stunt flying was thrilling because it was dangerous and killed many flyers.

In 1924 Amelia left California to move back east to Massachusetts where her mother and sister, now a teacher, had settled. Amelia, too, took up teaching for a while, joining the University of Massachusetts as an English tutor for newly-arrived **immigrant** factory workers. Many of her students were not only very poor but also bewildered by the experience of living in a strange new country. Amelia's concern for their problems led her to give up teaching and become a social worker, living in the city of Boston at a settlement called Dennison House.

Amelia still managed to keep up her flying, helping Bill Kinner sell his aeroplanes by demonstrating them to possible customers at Dennison Airport, near Squantam, Massachusetts. On one occasion she even managed to combine her two careers by flying over Boston to shower the city with leaflets advertising a fund-raising fair for Dennison House. Amelia had endless enthusiasm for flying, but, as yet, no idea how she could make it her full-time career.

One woman who did have a clear ambition was Amy Phipps Guest. Like Amelia, she had caught the flying bug. Unlike Amelia, she had a great deal of money. She wanted to be the first woman to cross the Atlantic Ocean by air. So she bought herself a three-engined Fokker aeroplane. Unfortunately for Mrs Guest, her family had other ideas and absolutely forbade the attempt. So Mrs Guest decided to find another woman to go in her place and she asked her friend George Putnam to help her find the right one.

George Putnam was a publisher and in the course of his work he met many people. But it was an explorer, Richard E Byrd, who first put forward Amelia Earhart's name. Putnam and his friends knew that whoever made the trip across the Atlantic would not only need to be physically fit and know a great deal about flying, they would also have to be able to cope with the publicity which would undoubtedly follow.

Would Amelia Earhart be spoiled by fame? They met her and decided she would not. So they offered her a unique chance to become an overnight celebrity and Amelia eagerly accepted. But fame was not the attraction for her. It was the experience itself which drew her.

"How could I refuse such a shining adventure?"

Commander Richard E Byrd (second left) with his flying crew, who became the first men to fly over the South Pole.

Charles Lindbergh and the
Spirit of St Louis

In 1919, following Alcock and Brown's first transatlantic flight from Newfoundland to Ireland, a French businessman, Mr M Orteig, offered a prize of $25,000 for the first successful flight, in either direction, between the United States and France – a distance almost twice as far as that flown by Alcock and Brown.

Mr Orteig's prize was not to be claimed until May 1927, when a 25-year-old mid-Westerner, Charles A Lindbergh, made the first ever solo flight across the Atlantic. Filled to the brim with fuel but without a fuel gauge or a radio, his specially-modified aeroplane *Spirit of St Louis* staggered into the sky at Roosevelt Field, Long Island, New York, barely clearing the trees at the end of the runway, and turned north towards Newfoundland. From there, Lindbergh headed west into the unknown, sometimes flying as high as 3,000 metres (10,000 feet) above the waves, with only home-made sandwiches to eat.

Ready for take-off on his historic flight, Lindbergh is helped into his overalls.

Lindbergh finally touched down before a crowd of 100,000 people at Le Bourget Airport, Paris at 10.24pm on 21 May 1927, having completed a flight of 5,760 kilometres (3,600 miles) in 33 hours and 39 minutes at an average speed of 172 kilometres (107.5 miles) per hour.

Lindbergh's welcome in France was **tumultuous**. Yet greater things awaited him at home. The American president dispatched a warship of the US Navy to bring home man and machine in triumph and Congress presented him with the Medal of Honour – the highest military decoration the United States can give.

An American hero – Lindbergh stands beside the *Spirit of St Louis* which took him across the Atlantic and to fame.

Left: **Centre of attention – Amelia outshines helmeted pilot Wilmer Stultz at their arrival at Southampton.**

Below: **Amelia at the door of the seaplane, *Friendship.***

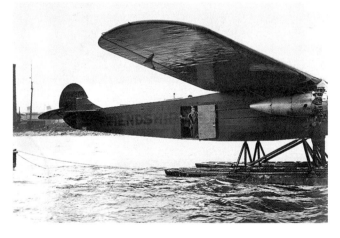

On 17 June 1928 Amelia Earhart joined pilot, Wilmer Stultz, and mechanic, Lou Gordon on board the *Friendship* at Trepassey Bay, Newfoundland. Their flight was to last 20 hours and 40 minutes. Amelia's job was simply to keep the log, noting down details of their speed, height and navigational directions. But when the *Friendship* at last set down at Burry Port, Wales, it was the tall, blonde girl with grey eyes that the newspapermen wanted to talk to and photograph. Amelia was careful to stress that she had not piloted the aeroplane, but to the eager public she was the heroine all the same.

What made Amelia Earhart such an attractive figure? Part of the attraction lay in flying itself. Aviation was still seen as a dangerous adventure and not just another form of transport. It was certainly not something many people would expect a young girl to be involved in. World War I had helped younger women to challenge firmly-held ideas about what women should and should not be expected or even allowed to do. In the service of their countries they had not only nursed the wounded but had driven them in ambulances under fire. In industry they had learned to handle heavy machinery and develop skills previously seen to be possible only for men to acquire. Many had gained a new self-confidence and wanted greater freedom in their daily lives. What could be a better symbol of freedom than to fly?

The fashions of the 1920s clearly showed this changed outlook. The style was positively boyish and Amelia Earhart, dressed in flying gear, was a brilliant example of the "new woman" who defied not only convention, but gravity itself.

In fact Amelia paid careful attention both to her appearance and the impression it gave of her.

All-American heroine – Amelia surrounded by London admirers.

She wanted to get people used to the idea of flying. If you were piloting an aeroplane from an open cockpit in cold weather you simply had to wear a bulky leather jacket with a helmet and goggles. But whenever she could do so she flew in an ordinary blouse and well-cut trousers and, when making public appearances, tried to avoid carrying a helmet and goggles. They suggested danger or at the least discomfort, and that was not the image of flying that she wanted to get across to the public.

Amelia liked to avoid being seen in stained and bulky overalls.

The young admired Amelia's courage, her skill and her cool, easy manners and tomboy looks. Older people, who often found the younger generation shocking, approved of the fact that she did not smoke, did not drink and did not boast.

The first ever transatlantic flight by a woman was celebrated in England with a round of formal receptions. When Amelia returned to the United States she found that she was already a household name and that the festivities were to be a good deal less restrained, with a **ticker-tape parade** down New York's Fifth Avenue and further parades in Boston and Chicago, both cities that could claim her as, in some small way, their own. On 17 December, moreover, Amelia was invited as an honoured celebrity to the special **commemoration** held at Kitty Hawk to mark the 25th anniversary of the Wright brothers'

historic flight.

Flyers called her "AE", but the press invented more fanciful names for her – "First Lady of the Air" and, in honour of Lindbergh, "Lady Lindy". Amelia herself joined the ranks of the writing profession when she wrote an account of her own historic flight. With characteristic simplicity she called it 20 Hrs. 40 Mins. She also became aviation director of Cosmopolitan magazine and took up lecturing as well. Another avenue opened up for her when she was appointed vice-president of Ludington Airlines, which later became National Airways. In keeping with her position as the symbol of the "new woman", she likewise became a leading figure in Zonta International, a service club for businesswomen and female professionals.

Amelia's most important commitment was to the 99s which

she helped to found in 1929. It began at a meeting of women attached to the sales staff of the Curtiss-Wright Company, an aeroplane manufacturers, on Long Island. Their aim was to create some sort of all-women's association. Some members just wanted a sort of social club. Others wanted a group to help them find work as professional flyers. But Amelia, as a strong believer in total equality for women, wanted an organization which would open up new opportunities and make sure that women had the same chances as men. They suggested that they take a number as their name. The number would be the amount of women who were prepared to pay their dues and sign up, and so the 99s were born. Soon they had their own magazine – "99er" with its own gossip column "Planely Personal", dress feature "Fashions in Flight" and cooking

advice "Pots and Pan Mechanics". Amelia served as President of the 99s until 1933.

None of these new commitments, however, dimmed her love of flying itself. In 1929 she took part in the first ever Women's Air Derby from Santa Monica, California to Cleveland, Ohio.

Races and records attract the attention of the press but demonstrating and selling aeroplanes was a far more regular activity for most women pilots. Amelia, already a heroine and a walking news event herself, was an ideal saleswoman. The Mono Aircraft Company, for example, was happy to lend her an aircraft free, in return for a four week tour in which she flew from town to town, stopping over to talk to local leaders and womens' groups while the sales force went around giving out brochures and talking to possible customers.

Amelia's casual dress suggests her relaxed attitude to flying.

George Putnam

George Palmer Putnam was a successful publisher and a married man with two sons when he first met Amelia Earhart in 1928. In 1930 he divorced his wife and on 7 February 1931 at Noank, Connecticut, married Amelia Earhart.

Settling in Rye, New York, the couple formed a successful partnership. He not only organized all the details of her flights and public appearances but also helped her use her name to **endorse** a range of flight luggage and a line of sports clothes. As a professional publisher he arranged for the publication of two of her books – *The Fun Of It*, which appeared the year after their marriage and *Last Flight*, which came out after her disappearance. In 1939 he wrote a biography of his late wife, *Soaring Wings*.

After her marriage to George Putnam, Amelia could have settled for a life of wealthy ease.

The Record Breaker

Success had not spoiled Amelia Earhart but she herself did not feel that she had earned it. On 21 May 1932 she set out to prove herself, for her own satisfaction, by trying to become the first woman to fly solo across the Atlantic. Piloting a Lockheed Vega monoplane she became not only the first woman to fly the Atlantic alone but also the first person in history to make the crossing by air more than once. Her record-breaking flight took her from Harbor Grace, Newfoundland to Culmore, Ireland and lasted just over 15 hours. Her achievement was acknowledged with a shower of awards – The Harmon International Trophy, the Distinguished Flying Cross from the US Congress, the cross of the French Legion of Honour and the gold medal of the National Geographic Society.

Above: **Landing in Ireland after her solo Atlantic flight.**

Below: **The monoplane in which Amelia made her solo Atlantic crossing.**

Yet more was to come. It was not that Amelia Earhart wished to add to her own reputation. Her place in the history books was already secure. But she was convinced that by constantly taking on new challenges in the air she could not only make it possible to learn new lessons that would make aviation even safer, but would also help people to realize that flying was more than just a novelty.

In 1933, on the 30th anniversary of the air age, the Franklin Institute in Philadelphia decided to honour the birth of the aeroplane with a special exhibition. The star exhibit was the Lockheed which Amelia had used the year before to cross the Atlantic and can still be seen there. At the opening ceremony Amelia herself gave the main lecture, tracing the 30-year history of manned flight, praising its beauty and predicting its bright future.

In 1935 Amelia made the first solo

America's ambassador, Andrew Mellor, welcomes Amelia to the American Embassy in London where she stayed until her return to the United States.

Amelia's exploits made her a household name on both sides of the Atlantic.

flight from Honolulu, Hawaii, to the American mainland, winning a $10,000 prize put up by Hawaiian businessmen keen to develop closer links with the United States. In the same year she also became the first person to fly non-stop from Mexico City to Newark, New Jersey.

Amelia Earhart's achievements and public behaviour had made her what nowadays would be called a "role model", someone that the younger generation should be encouraged to admire and imitate.

Amelia took her position in the public eye seriously and, in June 1935, at the request of Edward C Elliott, President of Purdue University, she agreed to become a careers adviser to its women students. She also accepted a position as the university's expert on aeronautics.

One week in every four, therefore, she would visit the university at Lafayette, Indiana, and stay in a student dormitory, mixing with the girl students and involving herself in research into the problems of designing better aircraft. Purdue's interest in aviation went even further as the university built its own airport and offered students flying lessons at reduced rates. As an expression of the value and commitment they placed in Amelia's expertise as a flyer, the trustees of Purdue established a special fund for aeronautical research and used it to buy her a modern Lockheed Electra.

Teaching by example – millions of young women saw Amelia as the ideal of independence.

In 1936 Amelia used her new aeroplane to take part in the Bendix Trophy air race, a speed dash from Floyd Bennet Field on Long Island, New York, to Mines Field in Los Angeles. The prize money totalled $15,000. The winners, from a field of seven, were veteran women pilots Louise Thaden and Blanche Noyes. Laura Engalls, flying solo, came second. Amelia and her co-pilot, Helen Richey, came in fifth. Women

Interior of the Vega – stripped of seats to make way for fuel tanks.

had taken three places out of the first five.

Amelia's Lockheed was so well kitted-out with every kind of new instrument that she nicknamed it "The Flying Laboratory". With such a machine at her disposal she began to prepare for "just one more long flight" – right round the world.

Flight Into History

Amelia crossing the Golden Gate Bridge, San Francisco.

Below: **A burst tyre wrecked this take-off from Honolulu.**

Amelia Earhart's last flight was planned for research, not records. The idea was to use the "Flying Laboratory" to study how high altitudes, long distances and extreme temperatures affected both aeroplanes and the people who flew in them, as well as to gather scientific data about the weather and to examine airport facilities in different countries.

On 17 March 1937 Amelia Earhart left Oakland, California intending to fly to Honolulu, with a crew of three – Captain Harry Manning, on leave from the *SS*

President Roosevelt; Frederick Noonan, an experienced pilot and navigator from Pan American Airways, and Paul Mantz, her technical adviser. They made it safely to Hawaii but a take-off accident then forced them to ship the aeroplane back to California for repairs. When the aeroplane was ready for a second attempt weather conditions forced a complete change of route and they decided to fly east instead of west.

On 1 June, 1937 Amelia Earhart left Miami, Florida, with Fred Noonan as her only crew. For a month they flew over oceans, deserts and jungles. Then, on 2 July, they set out on the most difficult leg of the whole journey, from Lae in New Guinea, to Howland Island in the middle of the Pacific Ocean – a distance of 4,089 kilometres (2,556 miles). The problem would be simply to find it. Howland Island was just three kilometres (two miles) long, less than one and a half kilometres (one mile) wide and only four and a half metres (15 feet) above sea level. But the US Coast Guard had built a landing strip there where they could refuel. And a Coast Guard **cutter**, *Itasca*, lay offshore waiting to guide them in by radio.

Amelia in Khartoum, Sudan on her fated round-the-world flight.

Less than 24 hours later, the *Itasca* began to pick up faint, scrambled messages from Amelia's Lockheed that their fuel was running low and there was no land in sight. The last incomplete message was received at 8.45am. The Lockheed Electra never got to Howland Island and, despite extensive searches by air and sea, no trace of its wreckage or its crew was ever found.

Top left: **No news – Amelia's mother waits by the radio hoping to hear news of her daughter's recent disappearance.**

Left: **Still hoping – George Putnam (centre) after weeks of searching.**

The laying of the foundation stone of the Earhart Memorial Light, Howland Island.

Many people refused to accept Amelia's fate. Privately-funded searches were mounted. After 1945 there were rumours that she had been on a secret spying mission; that she had been captured and executed by the Japanese; that she had flown off course and was still alive somewhere on a tiny Pacific Island. However, the most reliable evidence still suggests that Amelia Earhart was a victim of bad winds and weather who ran out of fuel within 160 kilometres (100 miles) of Howland Island, came down in the sea and was overwhelmed by waves.

Amelia Earhart was just 40 when she died. Her bravery, skill and enthusiasm inspired a generation of pilots and a generation of women. But even more important perhaps was the fact that, in the words of a tribute written shortly after her death, her extraordinary personality and deeds "made flying thinkable to so many people".

In July 1963 the United States issued a commemorative postage stamp, bearing her picture, to honour her memory. Fittingly it was for airmail use. In the same year a floating navigational light, bombed out during World War II, was restored to service on Howland Island and named, the Earhart Memorial Light. Even as you read these words it signals safety across a vast expanse of ocean – a bright and shining light, like the remarkable woman whose name it bears.

Find Out More ...

Important Books

20 Hrs 40 Mins by Amelia Earhart
  (G P Putnam's Sons, 1937).
Daughter of the Sky by Paul L
  Briand Jr (Duell, Sloan & Pearce,
  1960).
The Fun of It by Amelia Earhart
  (Brewer, Warren & Putnam,
  1932).

Last Flight by Amelia Earhart
  (Harcourt, Brace & Sons, 1937).
Soaring Wings by George Putnam
  (Harrap, 1939).

Important Dates

1897 Born, Atchison, Kansas
1907 Moves to Iowa
1913 Moves to Minnesota
1916 Graduates from high school in
      Chicago
1917 Volunteers for Red Cross
      service in Canada
1919 Enrolls at Columbia
      University
1920 Takes first flight
1921 Makes first flight;
      survives crash landing
1922 Buys first aeroplane
1924 Moves to Massachusetts

1926 Becomes a social worker
1928 Flies the Atlantic aboard
      Friendship
1929 Flies in first Women's Air
      Derby; founds the 99s
1931 Marries George Putnam
1932 Flies the Atlantic solo
1935 Makes first solo flight from
      Hawaii to mainland United
      States; joins Purdue
      University
1936 Flies in Bendix Air Trophy
      race
1937 Last flight.

Glossary

Commemoration In remembrance of a person or event.

Convalescing Recovering after an illness or injury.

Crop dusting Using aeroplanes to spray growing crops with chemicals to kill pests.

Cultivation Farming.

Cutter A small, high-powered boat.

Dispensary A clinic where medicines are made up and given out to patients.

Endorse To support or approve of.

Hangars Large sheds for storing aeroplanes under cover.

Immigrant Someone who has come to a new country intending to settle there.

Novice Someone new to a job or learning a skill.

Pawning Borrowing money in exchange for personal possessions with the chance to buy them back later.

Pneumonia A lung disease which can be fatal.

Reconnaissance Surveying an area to look for movements of troops.

Ticker-tape parade Before computers, information was sent to offices by telegraph and printed out on thin (one centimetre) strips of paper through "ticker" machines – thus "ticker-tape" waste was found in many offices; famous people were welcomed to cities by parading them in a procession which was showered with used ticker-tape from skyscrapers along their route.

Tumultuous Noisy and excited.

Veterans People who have been through a war or long period of hardship.

Index

Picture Acknowledgements

The publishers would like to thank the following for providing the photographs and illustrations in this book:
The Hulton Picture Library Frontispiece, 4 (top), 5,9,11,12,14,15 (bottom), 17 (right), 18,19,21 (both), 22,24,26 (top), 27,28 (top), 31: The Illustrated London News 8,20,23,29; Popperfoto 13,17 (left); The Royal Aeronautical Society 7 (bottom), 10; Topham Picture Library 6,7 (top), 15,16 (top), 25,26 (bottom), 28 (bottom); Zefa 4 (bottom).